Tim Tim and The Birthday Party Animals

Taylor Wyatt and Angelo Misseri

Illustrated By Steff Egan

Print ISBN: 978-1-7382205-0-2
eBook ISBN: 978-1-7382205-1-9

Illustrations by Steff Egan

Published By ToonGrin.com

Visit www.ToonGrin.com

Billy was a boy much like any other.
But Billy had anxiety and it gave him a stutter.
By the end of the week Billy would be six,
And the idea of his birthday was just making him sick.

His dads invited kids, all classmates from his school...
But Billy was worried he'd look like a fool.

He would think
"I'm too s-silly, too weird, and sh-shy."
"All everyone will see is a weirdo who c-cries."

"There's no need to feel scared,"
his dads spoke to their boy.
"But we hope this small present
will bring you some joy."
Now Billy tore through the paper
as careful as can be.
"What could my d-dads
have gotten for me?"

Billy looked deep inside
and now what did he see?
Not undies
or socks
but a
plush monkey.

"Billy, this is Tim Tim your brand-new best friend."
"Now, off you go! Play, son. And the fun will not end."
Tim Tim was cuddly, and his fur was so fluffy.
Billy could not believe that he could be so lucky.

The young boy loved Tim Tim with all of his heart.
Playing Games, Eating Lunch, they were never apart.

As the time flew by
Billy had such a blast.

But he knew his fun
with Tim Tim
could not last.

Because his birthday was here, and his head filled with fears.
He hugged Tim Tim tight and wiped up his tears.
Billy's dads went to comfort and
brighten his day.
"Don't worry,"
they said,
"It will
all be okay."

"Just hold Tim Tim tight,
when you feel scared."

"We will be
with your
Friends,
just
right
down
the
stairs."

So, Billy sat alone, feeling utterly blue.
He sat in his room thinking,
"What c-could I do?"

"W-who would be friends with someone like me?
I'm Alone
That's all I ever c-could be."

"Now don't say that!"
said a sweet and kind voice.
"When it comes to best friends, you're my very first choice!"
That voice? That sound?
Who on earth could it be?

Why it's Tim Tim!
His soft plush monkey!
Tim Tim was standing on his feet,
with a smile and a sway.
"I'm here to make this your Best Birthday!"

Billy sniffled, "Thanks, Tim Tim. But what c-can you do?"
"Making friends is im-possible" and he cried "Boo hoo!"

"All you need is
some practice,
for everyone
that's true.

So come along
with me Billy
and I'll show you
what to do."

Tim Tim walked Billy to a world of plush and wonder.
There were animals of all kinds, partying loud like thunder.
"Making friends can be scary.
You may not know what to do.
Let's try and make friends
as we go through this zoo."

At first Billy froze,
"N-NO!
There is simply no way.
I'm way too different from th-them,
what do you want me to say?"

Tim Tim held Billy's hand,
"I want you to take
a moment and breathe.
Take a good look.
Tell me, what do you see?"

Billy looked at all the animals, all Tim Tim's friends back-to-back.
From the nocturnal crew, the gorilla gang, and the petite pachyderm pack.

"Everyone has their quirks, their odds and their ends."
"Everyone is a bit odd, but we can still make new friends."
"You can find friends of all kinds. All different. All new."
"Just being yourself is all you need to do."

Billy then took a deep breath and closed his eyes tight.
And when he opened them up... everything was alright.

He could join in the party and dance all about
and with all his new friends Billy gave a big shout.
"I'm not too s-silly, weird or shy!"
"I can make friends too if I g-give it a try!"

"That's right!"
Tim Tim cheered, swinging down from a vine.
"If you open yourself up, you'll make friends in no time!"
"But it's time to go Billy," Tim Tim happily sighed.
"You have a party to go to. There is no need to hide."

The two said their farewells and returned to the door.
The animals said goodbye too. With a goodbye...

ROAR!!

Then the two tumbled from the closet, giggling with glee.
Billy was ready to make friends.
Thanks to Tim Tim,
his soft plush monkey.

So, he took a deep breath
and held Tim Tim tight.
Then ran downstairs

where it
would all
be alright.

Billy may still feel
worried, scared, and shy.
"But I can f-find friends too if I give it a try."
Because making friends can be hard, make no mistake.
But breaking the ice is easy,

with a little bit of cake.

Acknowledgements

Thank you to both of our family, friends and loved ones for encouraging and supporting us write this book and bring Tim Tim to Life. And to our dear reader, as you embark on this adventure with Tim Tim, know that your curiosity and imagination are the magic that brings these pages to life and are what make you amazing.

Thank you for being a part of this story.

May it bring joy and understanding to your heart.

About The Authors And Illustrator

Taylor Wyatt and **Angelo Misseri** are a duo with a country wide friendship who've decided to put their creative backgrounds and experiences into writing. Despite their great distance, they seek to write tales about empathy and understanding to celebrate the genuine kindness they wish to see more of in the world.

Steff Egan is an artist from Chicago who loves everything cute/fluffy and Tim Tim is no exception! While coming from a background in animation, Tim Tim is her first children's book. She was excited to collab on it as she would love to see kids have more access to books about anxiety and mental health.